Witness to History

The Rise of Hitler

Nathaniel Harris

www.heinemann.co.uk/library

Visit our website to find out more information about **Heinemann Library** books.

To order:

 Phone 44 (0) 1865 888066

 Send a fax to 44 (0) 1865 314091

 Visit the Heinemann Bookshop at www.heinemann.co.uk/library to browse our catalogue and order online.

First published in Great Britain by Heinemann Library,
Halley Court, Jordan Hill, Oxford
OX2 8EJ, part of Harcourt Education.
Heinemann is a registered trademark of
Harcourt Education Ltd.

Produced for Heinemann by Discovery Books Ltd
Editorial: Nancy Dickmann, Tanvi Rai and Helena Attlee
Design: Rob Norridge and Ron Kamen
Picture Research: Rachel Tisdale
Production: Séverine Ribierre

Originated by Dot Gradations
Printed and bound in China by South China
Printing Company

ISBN 0 431 17066 5
08 07 06 05 04
10 9 8 7 6 5 4 3 2 1

British Library Cataloguing in Publication Data
Harris, Nathaniel, 1937–
  The Rise of Hitler. – (Witness to History)
  943'.086'092

A full catalogue record for this book is available from the
British Library.

Acknowledgements
The publishers would like to thank the following for
permission to reproduce photographs: Corbis pp. **5, 6, 8,
13, 14, 15, 19, 30, 31, 32, 34, 35, 40, 41, 42, 43, 44, 45, 48,
51**; Peter Newark's Military Pictures pp. **10, 12, 17, 18, 20,
22, 24, 26, 28, 36, 38, 49**; Popperfoto pp. **16, 33, 46, 50**.

Cover photograph of Hitler saluting a huge crowd of Hitler
Youth at Nuremberg, c1930, reproduced with permission
of Corbis.

The publishers would like to thank Bob Rees, historian and
Assistant Head Teacher, for his assistance in the
preparation of this book

Every effort has been made to contact copyright holders of
any material reproduced in this book. Any omissions will
be rectified in subsequent printings if notice is given to the
publishers.

The paper used to print this book comes from
sustainable resources.

Words appearing in the text in bold, **like this**, are explained in the glossary.

Contents

Introduction

Adolf Hitler was the all-powerful **dictator** of Germany from 1933 to 1945, and for a time he ruled much of Europe. He, and the Nazi Party he led, suppressed Germany's **democratic republic** and permitted no opposition. Opponents were killed or imprisoned in brutal **concentration camps**, and the population was controlled through **propaganda** and terror. Hitler's policies led directly to World War II (1939-45) in which many millions of people died. Germany and its allies were eventually defeated and Hitler killed himself. The war devastated Europe, divided Germany, and had many other long-term effects that are still felt.

Hitler's dictatorship was based on a set of strange and repellent ideas. Many governments – including democratic governments – have behaved badly, failing to live up to their ideals. But in Hitler's Germany, concepts such as democracy and human rights were openly despised. The Nazis claimed that the Germans were a 'master race', entitled to destroy or enslave supposedly 'inferior' peoples. These ideas were most fully carried out during World War II, when the Nazis killed millions of people, either by working them to death or systematically murdering them.

By 1942, much of Europe was controlled by Germany and its allies.

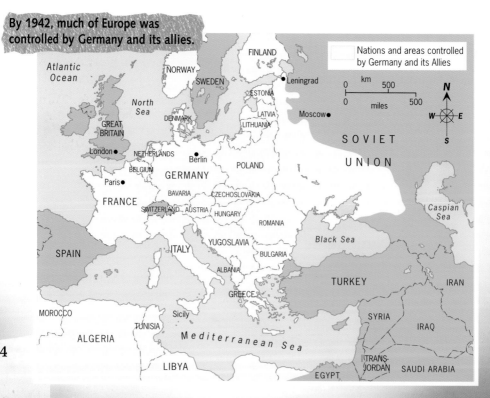

Savage messiah

Although Hitler was a **tyrant**, he had many followers. He was a powerful speaker who could whip a crowd into a frenzy, and a master of propaganda. But circumstances also helped him to rise. After Germany lost World War I (1914-18), many Germans felt they had been unfairly punished and humiliated by the victors. Then a brief recovery was followed by a worldwide **economic depression**. Germany was hard hit, and Hitler and the Nazis were able to use mass discontent to take power. Hitler's political skills enabled him to win support from wealthy people and out-manoeuvre political opponents.

Adolf Hitler, the all-powerful dictator, in 1934. He is arriving at a Nazi Party rally, surrounded by thousands of his followers displaying swastika banners and armbands.

Hitler made himself dictator, but he also succeeded in reviving the German economy. Germany was **rearmed** and became powerful again. Then, in the late 1930s, Hitler managed to acquire large territories abroad through a mixture of bluff and bullying, without going to war. These successes made it easy for many Germans to overlook the unpleasant side of Nazi rule. Hitler had begun to seem infallible, and when his policies did finally lead to war, German armies were victorious – until the tide turned and Germany was reduced to ruins.

How do we know?

The career of Adolf Hitler and the course of World War II are among the best known of all historical events. Thousands of books and articles have been written about them, ranging from general histories to studies of a single event or personality. Most of these works are **secondary sources**. In them, the authors give us their description of events and the conclusions they have drawn about them. These are usually based on an author's study of **primary sources**.

One form of historical evidence: papers issued during World War II, entitling the holder to buy **rationed** goods.

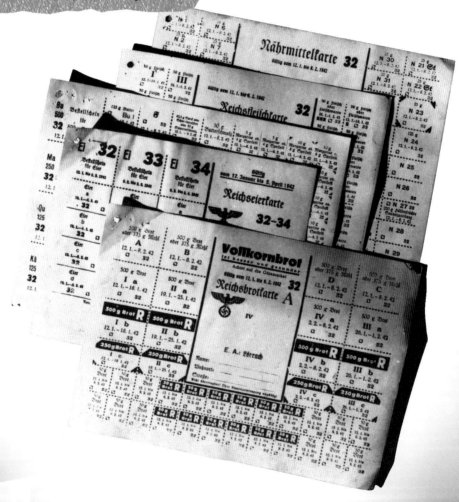

Primary sources consist of direct, first-hand evidence. Eye-witness accounts are particularly vivid primary sources, telling us what people saw and felt at a particular place and time. They may be found in books, letters, diaries, newspaper reports, and taped or filmed interviews. Photographs and newsreel films also provide eye-witness information, although in this case the eye is the eye of the camera. But there are many other types of primary sources, such as the texts of speeches, meetings and treaties, government documents, court records, and books and illustrations published during the historical period being studied. Even objects such as ration cards, badges and uniforms may tell us much about a society.

Assessing the evidence

This book presents a set of eye-witness accounts, records of speeches, and extracts from diaries written during the Hitler era. Eye-witness accounts help to bring a historical period to life. They give the reader a sense of how people of a different time felt, and they bring home raw realities like suffering and death. Events are sometimes easier to grasp through individual experiences – for example, the terror of a shoot-out (page 21), or the horror of being told casually that your mother has been murdered (page 43). However, any one eye-witness account, or similar source, may be misleading. For example, a single eye-witness may lie, distort or simply misremember. So it is important to be sure that a source is supported by many similar accounts or by information from separate sources.

Moreover, people living in the same society may not all have had the same experiences or shared the same views. Those who were able to live trouble-free under Hitler saw Germany in a different light from people who were persecuted by the Nazis. So the reader will find conflicting assessments of Hitler and different memories of his regime, even if its essentially evil nature is hardly in doubt.

Young Hitler

Adolf Hitler was born on 20 April 1889 at Braunau-am-Inn, but he spent most of his childhood in Linz. Both towns were in Austria, the German-speaking part of the Austro-Hungarian Empire. The empire itself was a huge, multinational state in central Europe where Germans, Hungarians, Czechs, Slovaks and other peoples lived together uneasily. Hitler's belief that the Germans were superior to all other peoples was certainly influenced by this background of national rivalries.

Gifted, but arrogant and undisciplined, Hitler had an unimpressive school career. He left at sixteen without any firm prospects, although he did dream of becoming an artist. But in 1907, when he went to Vienna, he twice failed to gain a place at the Academy of Fine Arts. When he ran out of money he had to live in a **doss house**. Later he managed to earn money by painting city views, and was able to live in a more comfortable hostel. He still felt a failure, and it was probably in Vienna that he became an ardent German **nationalist**, and began to blame Jews and non-Germans for his disappointments – and everything else.

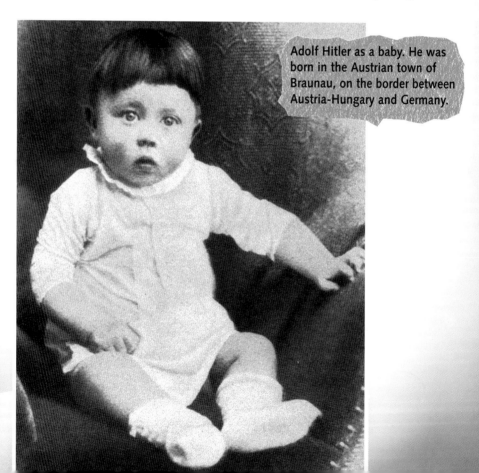

Adolf Hitler as a baby. He was born in the Austrian town of Braunau, on the border between Austria-Hungary and Germany.

Memorable child

Hitler was evidently memorable. Dr Eduard Hümer, one of his teachers, wrote this account of him in 1923.

I can recall the gaunt, pale-faced youth pretty well. He had definite talent, though in a narrow field. But he lacked self-discipline, being quarrelsome, headstrong, arrogant, and bad-tempered. He had obvious difficulty in fitting in at school. Moreover he was lazy, for otherwise, with his obvious gifts, he could hardly have failed to do well ... his enthusiasm for hard work evaporated all too quickly. He reacted with ill-concealed hostility to advice or rebuke; at the same time, he demanded of his fellow pupils their complete submission, fancying himself in the role of leader ...

Loving son

Dr Eduard Bloch was the Hitler family's Jewish physician. He attended Hitler's mother Klara during her last illness in 1907, and wrote this account in November 1938.

His attachment to his mother was deep and loving. He would watch her every movement so that he might anticipate her slightest need. His eyes, which usually gazed mournfully into the distance, would light up whenever she was relieved of her pain ... In all my forty-odd years of practice I had never seen a young man so broken by grief and bowed down by suffering as young Adolf Hitler was that day [of his mother's funeral, 23 December 1907].

World War I

In May 1913, Hitler moved to Munich, the most important city in the south German province of Bavaria. He was there when World War I broke out in August 1914. Like many people all over Europe, he was filled with **patriotic** enthusiasm; in his case, war service offered a new start. Although he was technically a foreigner in Germany, Hitler preferred to join the German army rather than the multinational Austro-Hungarian forces.

Germany and Austria-Hungary were **allies** in waging war on France, Russia, Great Britain and, later, the USA. The German plan to defeat France with a swift invasion did not succeed. For four years they were engaged in trench warfare, and the casualties were horrific. Hitler served on this front as a **dispatch runner**. It was highly dangerous work, and he was decorated for his bravery with the Iron Cross, First Class – an unusual award for a lowly **corporal**.

During 1918 the German army was pushed back, and in November an exhausted Germany asked for an **armistice**.

Hitler, on the far left of the photograph, with fellow-soldiers during World War I. He had a distinguished war record.

Defeat for Germany

In November 1918, Hitler was in hospital after being gassed. In the book he wrote in 1924, *Mein Kampf*, ('My Struggle') he described his feelings when he learned that Germany had lost the war.

I could stand it no longer. It became impossible for me to sit still one minute more. Again everything went black before my eyes; I tottered and groped my way back to the dormitory, threw myself on my bunk, and dug my burning head into my blankets and pillow.

Since the day when I had stood at my mother's grave, I had not wept. When in my youth Fate seized me with merciless hardness, my defiance mounted. When in the long war years Death snatched so many a dear comrade and friend from our ranks, it would have seemed to me almost a sin to complain – after all, were they not dying for Germany?... But now I could not help it. Only now did I see how all personal suffering vanishes in comparison with the misfortunes of the fatherland.

German troops in trenches on the Serbian frontier, 1915.

A defeated nation

World War I changed the map of Europe. In Russia, the **Bolsheviks**, or **Communists**, seized power and claimed to be establishing a workers' state. Poland, previously Russian-ruled, became independent. The Austro-Hungarian Empire broke up into a number of smaller states, including Austria, Hungary and Czechoslovakia (map page 4). When Hitler came to power, the creation of so many small, relatively weak East European countries would have important consequences.

In 1918 Germany was defeated and in great difficulties. The German emperor fled and a **democratic republic** was established. This became known as the Weimar Republic, from the name of the city where it was set up. The government of the new republic was faced with the job of officially making peace at Versailles in France. The Treaty of Versailles, imposed by the **Allies**, dealt harshly with Germany, which lost territory and was forced to **disarm**. It also had to admit its 'war guilt' and promise to pay compensation ('**reparations**') for the damage done to other countries during the war. Many Germans blamed the Weimar government for signing the treaty, though it had no choice. It then had to fight to survive against enemies at home. From 1919 onwards, a series of **uprisings** created great instability in Weimar Germany.

Post-war Germany

A young British writer, Douglas Goldring, wrote this account of the post-World War I atmosphere in Munich, the capital of the German province of Bavaria. Communists had held power for a few weeks, setting up a Bavarian Communist Republic. Now the Communists were being hunted by their bitter enemies, who hated Jews and other supposed 'traitors'. It was in turbulent Bavaria that Hitler began his political career.

At Munich I found myself in an atmosphere of tension. Kurt Eisner, head of the short-lived Bavarian Communist Republic, had recently been murdered ... and all the Commissars [officials] of the former **Red** Government were in hiding, and in danger of their lives. I stayed at the famous Vierjahreszeiten Hotel, where the **opulence** of the furniture and fittings contrasted with the patched sheets and towels, poor food and **ersatz** coffee. The people to whom I had introductions seemed frightened of talking to me, even in English. I called on a famous Jewish eye specialist and found him in a state of great agitation. He was expecting to be raided at any moment ... and was overcome with anxiety about the future fate of his wife and young daughter. When I went to see him again, two days later, deeply concerned by what he had told me, the blow had evidently fallen, for the house was closed and deserted. I was never able to discover what happened to these unfortunates, but concluded they were murdered like so many of their fellows.

Troubled times. Government troops in Berlin during the 1920 Kapp **Putsch**, an attempt to overthrow the new German republic.

Hitler the politician

When the war ended, Hitler returned to Munich, but he remained in the army. There were violent upheavals in the city, including a brief **Communist** government that was soon bloodily suppressed. The army authorities were strongly **nationalist** and anti-Communist. They trained political agents to win soldiers and citizens over to their views. Hitler was selected as one of these agents. He was soon training others, having discovered his great gift – the ability to speak fluently and passionately, thrilling and overwhelming an audience.

In September 1919, Hitler came into contact with a small political group in Munich, the German Workers' Party. He shared the extreme nationalist ideas of the party, and he soon joined it as member number 55. His gift for public speaking attracted many new recruits, and before long he became the party's leader. He showed a feeling for drama by introducing the outstretched-arm 'Roman' salute, adopting symbols such as the swastika (an ancient symbol of the sun), and forming military-style units of uniformed 'storm-troopers' (the SA). In February 1920, the German Workers' Party changed its name to the National Socialist German Workers' Party, or Nazi Party. For the time being, however, it was just one among a number of nationalist groups.

A man holding a Nazi flag during the early days of the movement. Hitler chose and designed many Nazi insignia.

Hitler's gift for public speaking

Hitler's forceful speaking mesmerized 19-year-old Hans Frank, who later became a leading Nazi. Frank refers to the Versailles Treaty as the 'Versailles Diktat' (dictated settlement) showing that many Germans felt that the treaty was forced upon them.

I was strongly impressed straightaway. It was totally different from what was otherwise to be heard in meetings. His method was completely clear and simple. He took the overwhelmingly dominant topic of the day, the Versailles Diktat, and posed the question of all questions: What now, German people? What's the true situation?... He spoke for over two-and-a-half hours, often interrupted by frenetic torrents of applause – and one could have listened to him for much, much longer. Everything came from the heart, and he struck a chord with all of us ... He concealed nothing... of the horror, the distress, the despair facing Germany. But not only that. He showed a way, the only way left to all ruined peoples in history, that of the grim new beginning from the most profound depths through courage, faith, readiness for action, hard work, and devotion to a great, shining, common goal ... When he finished, the applause would not die down ... From this evening onwards, though not a party member, I was convinced that if one man could do it, Hitler alone would be capable of mastering Germany's fate.

Hitler at a Nazi rally in 1928. Immediately in front of him stands Hermann Göring, ex-fighter pilot ace and Hitler's second in command.

Age of extremes

Radical political movements and ideas became important after World War I. They grew up where people became disillusioned with parliamentary politics and the way **capitalist** economies divided people into rich and poor. **Communist** Russia, renamed the Soviet Union or USSR, became the model for Communists everywhere. They aimed to overthrow their governments and take over the wealth, factories and other **economic** resources of their countries in the name of the workers. Social Democrats, or Socialists, were like the Communists in believing that societies needed to be fairer to working people. But they tried to bring this about peacefully, within the existing parliamentary system, rather than by violent revolution. Communists and Socialists are often described as **left wing**.

Right-wing movements fiercely opposed such changes. These movements also ranged from moderate **conservatives** to **extremists** – parties like Hitler's Nazis, which despised **democracy** and glorified force. Extreme right-wing movements also became very prominent after World War I. The first, in Italy, was Benito Mussolini's **Fascist** Party, which took power in 1922. The leader worship, military style and Roman salute of the Italian Fascists was copied by the Nazis and by similar, less successful parties that grew up in other countries. Such parties generally aimed at national expansion, usually through use of force.

Communist revolution in Russia. **Bolshevik** supporters demonstrate in front of St Isaac's Cathedral, Petrograd (now St Petersburg), in 1917.

Mussolini on Fascism

The Italian leader Benito Mussolini, an ex-journalist, wrote an article about Fascism that highlights its differences from democratic ideas and practices.

Faces of Fascism. This **propaganda** poster shows Benito Mussolini (top) and other leading Italian Fascists. The bundle of rods in the centre is an ancient Roman symbol of authority, the fasces, from which the movement took its name.

Above all, Fascism rejects the **doctrine** of **Pacifism** ...War alone brings up to their highest tension all human energies and puts the stamp of nobility upon the peoples... Fascism attacks the whole complex of democratic **ideologies** and rejects them ... Fascism denies that the majority can rule human societies ... it affirms the inequality of men.

Fascism desires the State to be strong … In the Fascist state the individual is not kept down, but rather multiplied, just as in a regiment a soldier is not weakened but multiplied by the number of his comrades. The Fascist state organizes the nation...it has limited useless or harmful liberties and has preserved those that are essential.

For Fascism the tendency to empire is a sign of health and strength; its opposite, staying at home, is a sign of decay.

But empire calls for discipline, co-ordination of forces, duty and sacrifice; this explains many aspects of the practical working of the **regime** and the necessary severity shown to those who oppose [it] ... peoples thirst for authority, for leadership, for order. If every age has its own doctrine, a thousand signs indicate that the doctrine of the present age is Fascism.

The great inflation

Although Germany's situation was unstable during the 1920s, the Weimar **Republic** survived. However, in January 1923 the Germans failed to keep up their **reparations** payments. French and Belgian forces punished them for this by occupying the Ruhr, a great German industrial centre. Germany could not fight back because it had been **disarmed** by the Treaty of Versailles. The Germans tried to undermine the occupation by arranging **strikes** among the factory workers. Unfortunately, it was the German **economy** that suffered.

1923: French troops occupy Germany's industrial heartland, the Ruhr, after the Germans failed to keep up their reparations payments.

Inflation (rising prices) soon became so extreme that German goods that had previously cost a few marks (German currency) began to be sold for millions. Workers were paid in wheelbarrow-loads of notes that they rushed to spend before their value fell even further. People's savings became worthless and many were ruined.

Coming after the sufferings of World War I, the great inflation convinced many people that ordinary political action was a waste of time. In this atmosphere, extreme ideas flourished. It looked as though an attempt to seize power by force might succeed, and Hitler decided to take the chance.

Marks by the million

An Austrian writer in Berlin, Stefan Zweig, witnessed the great inflation, and wrote this account in 1943.

Abruptly the mark plunged down, never to stop until it had reached the fantastic figures of madness, the millions, the billions and trillions. Now the real witches' sabbath [crazy performance] of inflation started ... to readers of today it would seem like a fairy tale. I have known days when I had to pay fifty thousand marks for a newspaper in the morning and a hundred thousand in the evening; whoever had foreign currency to exchange did so from hour to hour, because at four o'clock he would get a better rate than at three, and at five o'clock he would get much more than he had got an hour earlier ... On street-cars one paid in millions, lorries carried the paper money from the Reichsbank [the state bank] to the other banks, and a fortnight later one found hundred-thousand-mark notes in the gutter; a beggar had thrown them away contemptuously. A pair of shoe laces cost more than ... a fashionable store with two thousand pairs of shoes had cost before; to repair a broken window more than the whole house had formerly cost ... As marks were worthless, foreign currency became very valuable. For £20 one could buy rows of six-storey houses on Kurfürstendamm.

Money to burn. During the great inflation of 1923, a German woman uses worthless paper money to light the fire in her stove.

The Beer Hall Putsch

By 1923, Hitler's great skill as a public speaker had made him the undisputed leader of the Nazi Party. But he still needed the support of other **right-wing** groups if he was to take power in Bavaria. He arranged an alliance with Field Marshall Ludendorff, one of the most prestigious of wartime German generals. Hitler and Ludendorff planned to share the leadership of a **putsch** (sudden **uprising**) that would bring them to power.

The aim of the putsch was to take over Bavaria first and then march on Berlin, the German capital. Conditions seemed favourable, since **nationalist** feeling was strong in Bavaria, among the police and officials as well as ordinary people. Whether they would allow Hitler and Ludendorff to seize power remained to be seen.

On 9 November 1923, Hitler and Ludendorff led about 2500 armed men into Munich. Police units, even more heavily armed, blocked their path. Then a shot rang out and fighting began. The marchers had no chance against machine guns and armoured cars, and quickly dispersed. Hitler, injured in the confusion, was carried away by friends, but was soon arrested. The Beer Hall Putsch (so called because it was planned in Munich's beer halls) had failed miserably.

The Beer Hall Putsch. This painting by H. Schmitt is typical of Nazi propaganda. Hitler is the commanding central figure, and the failed revolt is shown as an heroic enterprise.

The police counterattack
Police Lieutenant Michael Freiherr von Godin took the decision to push back the marchers.

I went over to the counterattack against the ... Hitler people, with the order: 'Second Company, double time, march.'

I was received in their ranks with level bayonets, unlocked rifles, and levelled pistols. Some of my men were grabbed and had pistols held against their chests. My men worked with rifle-butt and night-stick ... Suddenly a Hitler man, who stood one step half-left of me, fired a pistol at my head. The shot went by my head and killed Sergeant Hollweg behind me.

Then, before I could give an order, my people opened fire ... At the same time the Hitler people commenced firing and for twenty or thirty seconds a regular fire-fight developed.

Death in the crowd
Josef Berchtold, one of the Nazi commanders, was in the thick of the action.

Everywhere people were going down, writhing on the ground in agony, dead and dying, while the guns still rattled death and murder into their stampeding midst. It was madness and slaughter.

Göring and Graf fell, badly wounded; fourteen dead were trampled under people's feet, throwing the living down; blood flowed everywhere over the grey pavement. The whole thing was a ghastly mess. Shrieks and cries filled the air, and ever that insane firing went on.

Nazi doctrine

Hitler was tried in front of sympathetic, **nationalist**-minded judges, and was finally sentenced to only five years in prison. There he dictated an account of his life and ideas, *Mein Kampf* ('My Struggle').

For Hitler, life was a pitiless struggle. He firmly believed that the Germans, supposedly a blue-eyed, fair-haired 'Aryan' people, were superior to all others. There was no scientific basis for this claim, or for his picture of Jews as vicious enemies of the Aryans. But **anti-Semitism** (hatred of the Jews) had a long history in Europe, so Hitler's ideas appealed to existing prejudices. He declared that the Jews were responsible for everything else that he hated – **democracy**, Socialism, **pacifism** and **Communism**. These 'Jewish' forces were also supposed to have betrayed Germany during the world war. The German army had not been beaten but 'stabbed in the back' by the politicians who had agreed to surrender – a myth that had a deep appeal to German pride. In the future, Hitler insisted, Germany must expand eastwards to acquire *Lebensraum* ('living space') in the territories occupied by 'inferior' East European peoples.

Hitler describes his ideas in *Mein Kampf*, which he wrote in 1924, while he was in prison. This cover, designed for a British translation of Hitler's book, is strongly anti-Nazi.

By rejecting the authority of the individual and replacing it by the numbers of some momentary mob ... majority rule sins against the basic aristocratic principle of Nature ... This invention of democracy is most intimately related to ... the cowardice of a great part of our so-called 'leadership' ...

If we pass all the causes of the German collapse in review, the ultimate and most decisive remains the failure to recognize the racial problem and especially the Jewish menace ... The lost purity of the blood alone destroys inner happiness forever, plunges man into the abyss for all time ...

We National Socialists ... take up where we broke off 600 years ago. We ... turn our gaze towards the land in the east ...

Here Fate itself seems desirous of giving us a sign ... If we speak of soil in Europe today, we can primarily have in mind only Russia and her vassal border states ... Impossible as it is for the Russian by himself to shake off the yoke of the Jew [i.e. the Communists] by his own resources, it is equally impossible for the Jew to maintain the mighty empire forever ...

Recovery and crisis

Hitler was released after only a year in prison. He had already decided on a change of tactics. The Nazis would have to win a place in government legally, by taking part in elections. Then the Nazi revolution could be carried out.

For most of the 1920s this seemed unlikely to happen. The **economic** crisis of 1923 passed. Germans became better off and enjoyed themselves. Former enemy states became less hostile, and wartime hatreds began to fade. **Extremist** parties like the Nazis do best in turbulent times, so Hitler and his followers made little progress.

But Weimar Germany's prosperity was dependent on American loans. In 1929 the loans were withdrawn because of the Wall Street Crash, a disastrous financial collapse in the US. It was followed by the world-wide Great Depression, during which factories and firms closed and people lost their jobs. Germany was particularly hard hit, with millions unemployed. Moderate politicians appeared to have no answer, and many people turned to the Nazi and **Communist** parties, which promised sweeping changes. As the crisis deepened, there was street fighting between different political groups, and the atmosphere became tense. In elections, the Nazi vote rose steeply. By July 1932, over 37 per cent of voters supported the Nazis.

Weimar culture. Arts and entertainment flourished in Germany during the 1920s. Berlin became celebrated for highly original and daring cabaret acts, which were small-scale performances put on in night-clubs.

The golden age of Weimar

A famous American journalist and historian, William L. Shirer, fondly recalled the 'golden age' of the Weimar Republic in the 1920s.

Life seemed more free, more modern, more exciting than in any place I had ever seen. Nowhere else did the arts or the intellectual life seem so lively ... And everywhere there was an accent on youth. One sat up with the young people all night in the pavement cafés, the plush bars, the summer camps, on a Rhineland steamer or in a smoke-filled artist's studio and talked endlessly about life. They were a healthy, carefree, sun-worshipping lot, and they were filled with an enormous zest for living to the full and in complete freedom ... One scarcely heard of Hitler or the Nazis except as butts of jokes – usually in connection with the [1923] **Putsch**.

Harry Kessler's diary

Count Harry Kessler, wealthy, liberal-minded and well-connected, described the decline of the Weimar Republic in his diary.

Berlin, Monday, 13 October 1930
The whole afternoon and evening mass demonstrations by the Nazis. During the afternoon they smashed the windows of Wertheim, Grünfeld, and other [Jewish-owned] department stores ... In the evening they assembled in the Potzdamer Platz, shouting 'Germany awake!' ... 'Death to Judah!' [the Jews] ... 'Heil Hitler!'... the Nazis consisted of adolescent riff-raff which made off yelling as soon as the police began to use rubber truncheons. I have never witnessed so much rabble in these parts ... These disorders reminded me of the days just before the [1918] revolution. If the Government does not take matters firmly in hand, we shall slide into **civil war**.

The takeover

Despite their successes, the Nazis never received enough support to be voted into power. Luckily for Hitler, he was able to make a deal with a **conservative** group that surrounded and influenced the president, Paul von Hindenburg. On 30 January 1933 he became **chancellor** (prime minister) of Germany. Apart from Hitler and his second-in-command, Hermann Göring, the conservatives held almost all of the important government posts. They were confident that they could 'tame' the Nazis.

A 1932 presidential election poster urging voters to support Hindenburg, who would, it was claimed, end the conflicts tearing Germany apart.

But Hitler now had all he needed – the power of the state behind him and a determination to use it ruthlessly. He had one stroke of luck when a mentally disturbed Dutchman burned down Germany's parliament building, the Reichstag. Hitler was quick to blame the **Communists** for this deed. He took the opportunity to arrest thousands of his **left-wing** opponents. Dachau, the first of many **concentration camps**, was opened to hold them. Now in control, the Nazis did well in new elections, and Hitler prepared his next move.

In March 1933 the Enabling Act was passed by the German parliament. This gave Hitler **dictatorial** powers for four years. He could now carry out his intention of making a Nazi revolution by using the power of the state. Within months, every **democratic** institution had crumbled, the Nazis controlled all the media, and non-Nazi political parties and trade unions were banned. The Weimar Republic was dead.

The police have at all costs to avoid anything suggestive of hostility to the SA, SS and Stahlhelm [Nazi and **nationalist paramilitaries**] as these organizations contain the most important constructive national elements. It is the business of the police to assist every form of national **propaganda**.

No mercy must be shown to organizations hostile to the State. Police officers who make use of fire-arms in the execution of their duties will, without regard to the consequences of such use, benefit by my protection; those who, out of a mistaken concern about these consequences, fail in their duty will be punished in accordance with the regulations.

Every official must bear in mind that failure to act will be regarded more seriously than an error due to taking action.

Saviour of the nation

The Nazi take-over was brutal. Many books with non-Nazi ideas were burned and there were mass arrests of political opponents. In 1934 there were even executions without trial of **dissident** Nazis, an incident that became known as the 'Night of the Long Knives'. Despite these shocking events, the Nazis' appeals for national unity impressed many Germans. When Hindenburg died in August 1934, Hitler took over the presidency, becoming Germany's **Führer** (leader) and **chancellor**. Nazi Germany became known as the **Third Reich**.

Hitler's future popularity would depend on his success in dealing with the **economic depression** and mass unemployment. Most countries had reacted to the crisis by cutting down on spending and lowering wages. It was later argued that governments should actually spend on big projects, employing as many workers as possible to get the economy moving again. Hitler adopted this approach, though for military rather than economic reasons. He launched a **rearmament** programme and commissioned the building of the first motorways, called *autobahns*. The number of unemployed fell sharply, and although living standards remained low, Germans had jobs again and were grateful for them.

Hitler, in the second window from the right, is hailed by crowds outside his official residence in Berlin after being appointed German chancellor.

Lloyd George's view

David Lloyd George, British prime minister during World War I, was impressed – and taken in – by 'the new Germany' after a visit in 1936.

I have just returned from a visit to Germany. There is for the first time since the War a general sense of security. The people are more cheerful. There is a greater sense of general gaiety of spirit throughout the land. It is a happier Germany.

As to his [Hitler's] popularity, especially among the youth of Germany, there can be no manner of doubt. The old trust him; the young idolize him. It is not the admiration accorded to a popular leader. It is the worship of a national hero who has saved his country from utter despondency and degradation.

It is true that public criticism of the Government is forbidden in every form. That does not mean that criticism is absent. I have heard the speeches of prominent Nazi orators freely condemned. But not a word of criticism or of disapproval have I heard of Hitler.

On the other hand, those who imagine that Germany has swung back to its old Imperialist temper cannot have any understanding of the character of the change. The idea of a Germany intimidating Europe with a threat that its irresistible army might march across frontiers forms no part of the new vision.

Life in the Third Reich

Nazi Germany was a totalitarian society – one in which every aspect of life was controlled by the state. Control was enforced by security police in black uniforms, the SS, and by a plain-clothed secret police, the Gestapo. But relentless **propaganda** was equally important. Books, newspapers and newsreels were all used to spread Nazi values, and the radio was especially important because it brought propaganda into the home.

The Nazis were also masters of 'political theatre'. This took the form of spectacularly staged parades and festivals like the annual Nuremberg Rallies. They were designed to give an overwhelming impression of power and unity. Ordinary people had a part to play in some of these and, according to one estimate, about a third of all Germans had a uniform of some kind.

Propaganda was designed to convince Germans that they were a united people, brought together by the **Third Reich**. Above all, they were told they owed everything to Adolf Hitler. The Nazi propaganda machine, directed by Josef Goebbels, pictured the **Führer** as an inspired, god-like being, with a kindly human side. Many Germans believed in 'the infallible Führer – almost to the end of Hitler's life.

Massed formations of storm-troopers, banners, floodlights: this night scene from the 1936 Nuremberg Rally was typical of the Nazis' mastery of spectacular effects.

Goebbels on Hitler

The cult of Hitler was promoted by the propaganda minister, Goebbels. One of many examples is Goebbels' preface to his book *Adolf Hitler – Pictures from the life of the Führer* (1936).

He [Hitler] has always instinctively understood how to speak and deal with his people ... From an early time, all the love and immense trust of his followers, and later of the whole of the German nation, has been focused on him. Yet initially the masses saw him from a distance only as a politician and statesman. His purely human side remained largely in the background.

Today the whole world recognizes him as the initiator of the National Socialist doctrine and the creator of the National Socialist state, the pioneer of a new European order and the guide to peace and the welfare of nations. But behind this recognition countless millions of people the world over suspect that there is a fascinating and compelling personality behind the front presented to the world by the man Adolf Hitler. Germans and non-Germans alike have been captured by the great simplicity and simple greatness which this man radiates.

In order to understand him completely, one must know him not only as a politician and a statesman, but also as a human being. It is to this end that the book has been written.

Dr Joseph Goebbels, Nazi minister of propaganda, giving a speech in 1945. His control of films, radio and newspapers strengthened Germans' belief in Hitler.

A united people?

Although **propaganda** idealized life under the Third Reich, for many Germans in the 1930s it did genuinely seem better. Millions remained grateful for their jobs, even though **strikes** were banned and they had few rights in their dealings with employers.

The Nazi state made well-publicized efforts to help the poorest people in society. They funded the party welfare organization and raised large sums through charity appeals. 'Volunteering' to help and making contributions were often made difficult to avoid.

BUND
DEUTSCHER
MÄDEL
IN DER
HITLER
JUGEND

Nazi doctrine stated that women belonged in the home as wives and mothers, not in the workplace. There were some exceptions, notably female doctors and nurses. Motherhood was praised and rewarded, and rest homes were built for new mothers. Their children attended **kindergarten** and, when old enough, joined organizations such as Hitler Youth and the German Girls' League. Here they enjoyed adventures, learned comradeship and, of course, Nazi values. Since no open opposition was allowed to stir up discontent, many people remained uninterested in politics. They concentrated on work or hobbies, boyfriends or girlfriends. Life was satisfactory – for those who were in step.

The propaganda state. Posters like these ('German Girls' League in the Hitler Youth') were a powerful form of Nazi propaganda, reinforced by radio broadcasts, newsreels, films, books and even popular songs.

German Girls' League

Gerda Klinger, born in 1920, proved to be a talented administrator. Her career, starting in the German Girls' League, showed how easily an ordinary, non-political person could become involved with the Nazi Party.

When I went on to high school ... we were taught by Nazi teachers who told us of the terrible injustices of the Versailles Treaty and the loss of our colonies, taken over by the **Allies** ... led by Jewish businessmen, corrupt lords in England and all sorts of greedy individuals ... All this was drummed into us ...not only in school but in the youth movement, which I joined as did almost every other child ...

In due course I was made a leader in the BDM [German Girls' League], and as such it was my job to look after ... discipline, hygiene, the role of women in the new Germany, the need to produce fine children and to support our menfolk in all things ...

One day I was asked to attend an interview at the Party HQ, and ... I leapt at this opportunity to advance myself ... I have to admit that. It seemed a very good idea at the time, and they had some good points, especially on the social side, for they always did their utmost to attend to the needs of the people, however much they failed in other ways.

Flying the flag. There were a number of Nazi organizations designed for young people, and pressure to join one of them was very strong.

Living in fear

Although many people were unaffected, life for some people in Nazi Germany was a nightmare. People were encouraged to **denounce** one another, and anti-Nazis were arrested and sent to **concentration camps**. Others lived in constant fear of arrest.

Non-Nazi ideas about history or science were outlawed. This meant that many writers and thinkers felt compelled to leave Germany. Any but the most conventional kind of art was ridiculed as '**degenerate**'.

Anyone who was not a healthy, useful 'Aryan' was likely to be badly treated by the Nazis, who virtually ignored the mentally disabled and incurably ill. When war came, these unfortunate people were simply killed. But the most consistently harsh actions of the **regime** were directed against the 600,000 Jews in Germany. By 1935 they had been stripped of their citizenship. They were driven out of professions like medicine, university teaching and the law. On 9-10 November 1938, Jews and Jewish properties were attacked all over Germany. This was known as *Kristallnacht* (Crystal Night) because so much glass was broken. Over 7500 Jewish businesses were destroyed and more than 26,000 Jews were arrested and robbed. About 80,000 left the country, but the great majority stayed, still hoping for better times.

Jewish shop windows after *Kristallnacht*, 9-10 November 1938, when beatings, murders and wrecking of property by Nazis were carried out all over Germany.

Under pressure, day after day

Victor Klemperer was a German Jewish university teacher. He had fought for Germany in World War I, and was less severely persecuted than some other Jews. But his ordeal was bad enough, as these diary extracts show.

'The new Germany', 1935: people who didn't fit in. Prisoners march under guard to a Nazi concentration camp.

10.3.1933. Day after day commissioners appointed, provincial governments trampled underfoot, flags raised, buildings taken over, people shot, newspapers banned, etc. etc... A complete revolution and party dictatorship. And all opposing forces as if vanished from the face of the earth.

31.3.1933. The Dresden student body made a declaration today: the honour of German students forbids them to come into contact with Jews. Jews are not allowed to enter the Student House.

10.4.1933. The new Civil Service law leaves me in my post — at least for the time being ... I hear nothing from my relatives. No one dares write.

27.1.1934. Note to Professor Klemperer: 'The Ministry has decided to cancel your appointment to the Examination Board.'

30.4.1935. I do not need to give a lecture, because I received my dismissal notice through the post.

21.7.1935. Jew-baiting ... Goebbels' speeches ('exterminate them like fleas and bedbugs!'), acts of violence in Berlin, Breslau, yesterday also here [Dresden] ... I truly expect that one day our little house will be set alight and I shall be beaten to death.

27.11.1938. Two policemen. Did I have any weapons? — Certainly my sabre, perhaps even my bayonet as a war memento, but I wouldn't know where. — The house was searched for hours.

6.12.1938. Withdrawal of all driving licences from Jews. New Jewish laws come out nearly every — no, really every day, so our nerves have gone to the dogs.

3.9.1939. As I lie down to sleep I think: Will they come for me tonight?

Unbroken successes

Hitler's prestige was enhanced by a series of foreign policy triumphs. He defied the Treaty of Versailles by **rearming** Germany. Then in 1936 he sent troops into the Rhineland. This was German territory, but it had been **demilitarized**. Hitler was bluffing, since Germany was not yet strong enough to fight Britain and France. But he rightly believed they would not act. They certainly wanted to avoid another war, and realized that Germany had been badly treated in the past.

In March 1938, Hitler used force and bullying to make Austria part of the **Third Reich**. Again, the union (*Anschluss*) of the two Germanic states, though forbidden at Versailles, seemed reasonable. Then he began a campaign against neighbouring Czechoslovakia, where 3 million Germans lived and were supposedly being persecuted. War appeared close for a time, but in September 1938 a conference at Munich (between Germany, Italy, Britain and France) gave Hitler large areas of Czechoslovak territory. Britain and France were following a policy of **appeasement** – trying to satisfy Hitler in order to avoid war. Hitler's advisers, including his generals, often disapproved of his foreign policy. But these events seemed to show that he really was a genius. He had restored Germany as a great power without firing a shot.

Triumphal march. In 1938 German troops 'goose-step' through Vienna following the *Anschluss* uniting Germany and Austria.

Germany takes over Czechoslovakia

Hitler's interpreter, Paul Schmidt, was present on 15 March 1939, when the Czech leaders were blackmailed into 'inviting' the Nazis into their country.

Hacha and Chwalkowski [Czech president and foreign minister] ... sought an interview with Hitler, who agreed to receive them in Berlin ...

In Hitler's gloomy office the realities of the situation emerged ... [Hitler declared that] for the security of the Reich, it was necessary for Germany to assume a protectorate over ... Czechoslovakia. Hacha and Chwalkowski sat as though turned to stone ... the end of their country had come. They had set out from Prague in the hope that they would be able to treat [negotiate] with Hitler but already they had been told that German troops had crossed their frontier.

... 'The German troops' entry can't be hindered', said Hitler. 'If you want to avoid bloodshed you had better telephone to Prague at once, and ... order the Czech forces to offer no resistance.' With these words Hitler brought the interview to an end ...

I was now busily preparing a fair copy ... of the communiqué [statement for the Czechs to sign]: 'The President of the State of Czechoslovakia has declared that ... he confidently lays the fate of the Czech people and country in the hands of the **Führer** ... The Führer has accepted this declaration, and has announced his decision to take the Czech people under the protection of the German Reich ...'

On the warpath

Hitler continued to move rapidly, and the rest of Czechoslovakia was soon brought under Nazi control. Then he made war on Poland. By this time, British and French leaders realized **appeasement** had failed. They gave their backing to the Poles and in September 1939 Britain and France declared war on Germany.

Despite his hatred for its 'inferior' Slav peoples and 'Jewish' **Communist** system, Hitler had signed a **non-aggression** pact with the leaders of the Soviet Union. Within weeks Germany and the Soviet Union had divided Poland up between them.

After a brief lull Germany went on to conquer Norway and Denmark in 1940, and then the Netherlands, Belgium and France. As in Poland, these spectacular *Blitzkriegs* (lightning attacks) were based on the combined use of tanks, infantry and air power to disorganize and destroy the enemy.

Fascist Italy now sided with Nazi Germany, and Britain stood alone in Europe against them. But plans to invade Britain were shelved after the Royal Air Force defeated the Germans in the air during the Battle of Britain in 1940. Instead, Hitler turned on the Soviet Union. On 22 June 1941, without any declaration of war, German forces invaded, smashing Soviet armies and conquering vast territories.

The invaders, September 1939. These German troops have entered Poland; the road sign indicates that they are 347 kilometres (216 miles) from the Polish capital, Warsaw (Warszawa).

On or about August 10, 1939, the chief of the SD [intelligence service], Heydrich, personally ordered me to simulate an attack on the [German] radio station near Gleiwitz near the Polish border and to make it appear that the attacking force consisted of Poles. Heydrich said: 'Practical proof is needed for these attacks of the Poles for the foreign press as well as for German **propaganda** …'

My instructions were to seize the radio station and to hold it long enough to permit a Polish-speaking German who would be put at my disposal to broadcast a speech in Polish …

…12 to 13 condemned criminals … were to be dressed in Polish uniforms and left dead on the ground of the scene of the incident to show they had been killed while attacking. For this purpose they were to be given fatal injections … Then they were also to be given gunshot wounds. After the incident members of the press and other persons were to be taken to the spot …

Occupied Europe

At its height, Hitler's empire stretched from the Atlantic to the gates of Moscow, the Russian capital. Among the conquered peoples, there were groups with similar ideas to the Nazis, and many of these became **collaborators**. But essentially Hitler believed in ruling through force and fear. Though it made the Nazis hated, conquered countries were ruthlessly exploited. In Western Europe, the Nazis behaved reasonably well at first. But resistance was punished by brutal **reprisals** such as shooting hostages and destroying entire villages. This only provoked fiercer opposition. In rugged countryside, bands of **partisans** waged hit-and-run warfare against the Germans. Elsewhere, resisters worked in secret, distributing anti-Nazi leaflets and committing acts of **sabotage**. Many members of the French Resistance fell into the hands of the Gestapo and suffered torture and death.

In the East, there were no pretences: Hitler told his generals to wage 'a war of **annihilation**'. Polish and Russian civilians were starved and degraded. Death squads committed mass murders, and millions of Soviet prisoners of war were worked to death as slave labourers.

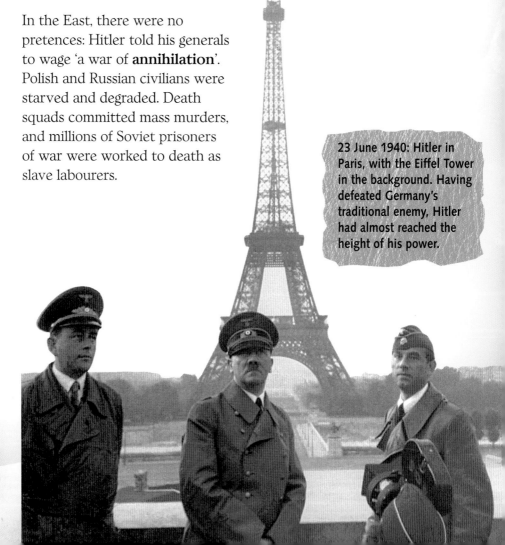

23 June 1940: Hitler in Paris, with the Eiffel Tower in the background. Having defeated Germany's traditional enemy, Hitler had almost reached the height of his power.

Fighting in the Resistance
A Frenchwoman, Anne-Marie Bauer, described her work fighting for the French Resistance against German occupation.

I was driving trucks and ambulances when my brother, Etienne, asked me to join him in a [resistance] movement called Libération. I went to work at first in Montpellier, distributing tracts and telling young Frenchmen not to ... work in Germany. Then I met Paul Schmidt and Gérard Brault ... They asked me to join them and help in organizing parachute operations and landings of Lysander planes [small British planes]. My job was to scout out good landing fields, flat enough and of the right length and width, and far enough from populated places or enemy observation ...

We not only found many, many landing sites, but also set up a team of smugglers. I took dozens of photos and measurements and brought it all to Schmidt, who gave it to [Resistance leader Jean] Moulin.

They were delighted with my work and congratulated me, but when, a month later, a para[chute] drop was scheduled for my field, they wouldn't let me go. Said it was too dangerous for a woman. They sent my brother, Etienne, instead. I was enraged and told them that I'd go to the next drop or they wouldn't get any more locations from me. They gave in.

French Resistance fighters marching along a mountain track in 1944.

War on the weak

Mothers and children arriving at the Auschwitz death camp; each wears the yellow star compulsory for all Jews. Almost all of them will certainly die.

In Eastern Europe, the Nazis committed the most infamous of all their crimes – their campaign to **exterminate** the Jews. This is now known as the Holocaust (fiery destruction). Many thousands were shot down by death squads operating behind the lines in Poland and Russia. But even massacres were judged to be too slow. At a conference in early 1942, the Nazis decided on a systematic, mechanized 'Final Solution' that would eliminate all the Jews under their rule. Auschwitz and other death camps were set up in the East.

Unlike concentration camps, the death camps had equipment for gassing victims in large numbers and ovens to burn the bodies. Jews were rounded up everywhere from France to Romania and transported via the European railway network to the camps. There, those who could not work were gassed straight away; those who were fit enough were worked until they were 'useless' and were then gassed. Of the 6 million Jewish men, women and children killed by the Nazis, the majority perished in the camps, along with others hated by Hitler and the Nazis: gypsies, members of the Resistance, homosexuals, **Communists**, and anti-Nazi church leaders.

Arrival at Auschwitz

Lidia Rosenfeld Vago, a Hungarian Jew, described being taken to Auschwitz. She was separated from her mother, who could not work and so was killed on arrival.

Not for a moment did my sister and I fear extermination. It was beyond our wildest pessimistic fantasies ... We entered a large hall in which several women barbers (not hairdressers) were set up. Working as if in a race against time, they rudely cut our hair, leaving us bald and clean-shaven everywhere on our entire bodies. The culture shock proceeded as our female bodies were stripped and exposed to the gaze of the German soldiers ... We were marched to our lodgings, a huge barren compound surrounded by electric barbed wire, with rows upon rows of rudimentary wooden huts, most of them unfinished ... The huts had no bunks, just the wooden floor and an unfinished, leaking roof.

I tried to approach our blockowa [a veteran inmate who was in charge]. 'Where are our mothers, children, and grandparents?' [She] pointed toward dark clouds of smoke with flames shooting up here and there in the distance. 'There are your mothers and children going up in smoke just now.' ... Most of the girls from our group of about one thousand were found fit for 'extermination through work'. Then we were taken to the sauna again, where we were branded ...

Maidanek death camp, Poland, in August 1944. This huge heap of shoes, carefully put aside by the Nazis, belonged to some of the men, women and children who had been murdered there.

A change of fortune

Despite their successes, the German forces failed to destroy the USSR.
Instead of a rapid victory, Hitler faced a long, merciless struggle.
Meanwhile, on 11 December 1941, he declared war on the United
States. The USA had just been attacked (on 7 December 1941)
without warning by Japan, an aggressive state friendly to Nazi
Germany. The USA had been giving Britain much unofficial help
against Germany, and Hitler was convinced that it would enter the
war soon. So, typically, he preferred to take the initiative.

7 December 1941: an American
warship explodes during the Japanese
attack on Pearl Harbor. Hitler's
support for Japan turned the huge
resources of the USA against him.

Nevertheless it was a fatal mistake. In the long run, the combined
resources of the USA, Britain and the USSR were bound to prevail. In
1942-3 the war gradually turned against Germany in the Atlantic, in
North Africa and, above all, in Russia. In January 1943, an entire
German army that had been attacking Stalingrad was surrounded and
forced to surrender. In July, another German offensive was halted
after the greatest tank battle of the war, at Kursk. Now the Soviet
forces began a slow but relentless westward advance.

The Russian front

In the summer of 1942, Paul Stresemann was a bridging engineer in his early thirties, serving with the German Army on the Russian front.

We had been driving all day and were filthy, hot and very thirsty and hungry. At last we reached our bivouac [camp] area, but had only just settled down to eat some food when the Russian artillery hit us. We were caught by surprise, in the open really with very little shelter, and took **casualties** at once. The explosions were very loud and I saw men, horses and trucks go flying up into the air in all directions ... I fell into a large hole or crater and the shelling went on for some time.

When it stopped and I dared to look out of my hole I saw a scene of utter desolation. All the horses and trucks and equipment were wrecked and only here and there a surviving soldier, as dazed as I was. We tried to assemble and pick up the pieces, but it was no use. We were sent as survivors to the rear. It was the end of our old unit and, in fact, I was the only survivor of the original bunch of men who had started out in Poland.

The beginning of the end. Frozen and half-starved German prisoners march into captivity at Stalingrad, January 1943.

The crumbling fortress

The war in the East absorbed most of Hitler's energies. In December 1941, unhappy with his generals, he assumed direct command of the armed forces. He now rarely appeared in public, working in his headquarters, the 'Wolf's Lair', in northern Poland. As a military leader, he believed in never retreating and, where possible, taking the initiative and attacking. On occasion he made good decisions, but as the balance of forces turned against Germany, his fixed attitudes cost many German lives.

Meanwhile, life grew harder on the German home front. The production of non-essential goods was cut back and women were brought into the work force. German civilians felt the full impact of war as superiority in the air passed to the **Allies** and bombs began to rain down on cities and factories.

Though Hitler's reputation for infallibility had been damaged, few dared to show any signs of discontent. German-dominated Europe was still formidably defended. But in June 1944 it was breached in the west when American and British forces successfully landed on the beaches of Normandy in France.

Tragedy at the kindergarten

A widowed mother in Cologne, Käthe Schlecter-Bonnesen, recalled what happened after she left her two children in a **kindergarten** for safety, only to find it had been hit in an Allied air raid. It is clear that she blamed the Nazis, not the Allies, for starting the war.

At first I looked in the bunker where the children went during an alarm, but I didn't find them. I saw other children, but I couldn't find my own two ... Later, I heard that a whole group of people had been buried in a house in Nibelungen Street, including children from the kindergarten ... More and more people were pulled out of the cellar of that house ... My two children were pulled out dead. You could hardly see any injuries on them. They only had a small drop of blood on their noses and large bloody scrapes on the backs of their heads.

I was in a state of total shock. I wanted to scream, right then and there I wanted to scream, 'You Nazis, you murderers!' ... A neighbour, who had only been released from a **concentration camp** a few days before, grabbed my arm and pulled me aside. He said, 'Do you want to get yourself arrested, too?'

Düsseldorf in ruins. As the war gradually turned against Germany, Allied bombing devastated most of the country's cities and industrial centres.

The end

After the Normandy landings, Nazi Europe was under attack from every direction. All but the most fanatical Nazis could see that the war was lost. Hitler's determination to fight on only caused unnecessary suffering and death.

A group of German officers and civilians planned to assassinate Hitler on 20 July 1944 and take power from the Nazis. But when Colonel Claus von Stauffenberg planted a bomb at the Wolf's Lair, Hitler survived. The conspirators were executed, and Hitler, though increasingly aged and broken, remained in complete command.

Hitler was determined to fight 'Jewish Bolshevism' to the end and, if he fell, was prepared – perhaps wanted – to see Germany destroyed with him. A final offensive (the Battle of the Bulge, in the Ardennes, Belgium) failed and the **Allies** advanced rapidly into Germany itself. Hitler's last wild hopes faded as Soviet troops entered Berlin, where he and his staff were living in an underground bunker. Even in his final hours, Hitler blamed his ruin on treacherous followers or the German people – everyone but himself. On 30 April 1945, he and his long-time companion Eva Braun were married and then killed themselves.

A US soldier guards German prisoners in April 1945, shortly before the Nazi surrender.

Germany destroyed

Just before the end, Albert Speer, German armaments minister, found Hitler in the mood to drag Germany down with him. Hitler felt that, if the Germans had lost, they did not deserve to go on living.

I felt rather uneasy ... I could feel his ill humour as he dismissed me and [I] was already at the door when he said, as if cutting out the possibility of any answer: 'This time you will receive a written reply to your memorandum!' [opposing the destruction of factories and other vital German resources to keep them from the advancing Allies] ... He made a brief pause, then in an icy tone continued: 'If the war is lost, the people will be lost also. It is not necessary to worry about what the German people will need for elemental survival. On the contrary, it is best for us to destroy even these things. For the nation has proved to be the weaker, and the future belongs solely to the stronger eastern nation [the Soviet Union]. In any case, only those who are inferior will remain after this struggle, for the good have already been killed.'

The final days. An aged-looking Hitler congratulates the 12-year-old winner of the Iron Cross – one of many young boys recruited in 1945 to defend the crumbling Reich.

What have we learnt from the rise of Hitler?

The war in Europe – and the **Third Reich** – ended within days of Hitler's death, although his Japanese allies fought on for a few months. Germany surrendered unconditionally on 7 May 1945. Over 40 million people are believed to have died in World War II. Afterwards there was a strong feeling that nothing like this must be allowed to happen again. An international court was set up at Nuremberg to try and punish Nazis. The United Nations was founded so that states could peacefully discuss their differences.

But other consequences of Hitler's career led to new problems. Germany was divided. The USSR set up **Communist** states in former Nazi territories that it had conquered in Eastern Europe, including East Germany. Wartime alliances dissolved and there was increasing hostility between a US-led alliance and Communist powers. As a result, post-Nazi Europe was divided for almost 50 years.

The United States had once been inclined to ignore the rest of the world, but it now became permanently involved in international politics. And in time France formed a partnership with a new, **democratic** West Germany that eventually evolved into the European Union. These are just of few features of the modern world that came out of the rise, and especially the fall, of Adolf Hitler.

In 1961 the Communist part of Berlin was sealed off by a wall that remained up until 1989. The division of Berlin, and of Germany, was a legacy of the Hitler period.

Educating the young

Martin Bormann, the son of one of Hitler's most trusted followers, almost committed suicide when he heard of Hitler's death. But later he became a priest and taught children about the evils of Nazism.

I don't have to invent or even describe ... I just read them bits from Hitler's speeches, about the teaching of the young. 'I want no intellectual education', Hitler said. 'Knowledge will spoil the young for me. It is control they must learn; it is the fear of death they must conquer: this is what creates true freedom, creativity and maturity for the young'. When I read this to boys and girls now ... and tell them how Hitler owned us from the age of ten, and how, he said, going from *Pimpf* [a junior youth organization] to Hitler Youth, to Workers' Front, into the SS, SA and *Wehrmacht* [German army] would make us his for ever, they can identify with what he was. They can relate it to their own so very different lives and understand ... this one-man **dictatorship** which we, who were all his and never free, never could ... Our plans for the world were so wide-reaching, and so terrible, that we can only thank God we lost the war.

Hermann Göring (far left) and other leading Nazis who survived the war are shown in court at Nuremberg in Germany. They were put on trial and most were convicted, executed or imprisoned for war crimes.

51

Timeline

1889   Adolf Hitler born on 20 April at Braunau-am-Inn, Austria.

1907   Hitler goes to Vienna, where he fails to get into Academy of Fine Arts. His mother dies in December.

1913   May: Hitler moves to Munich.

1914   August: World War I breaks out.

1918   November: end of World War I. Hitler is in hospital recovering from war injuries. Germany becomes a **republic**.

1919   September: Hitler joins the German Workers' Party.

1920   February: the German Workers' Party becomes the National Socialist German Workers' (Nazi) Party.

1922   Mussolini's **Fascist** Party takes power in Italy.

1923   French and Belgian forces occupy the Ruhr. Hitler becomes undisputed leader of the Nazi Party. 9 November: the Munich **Putsch** fails and Hitler is arrested.

1924   Hitler writes *Mein Kampf* in prison. He is released on 20 December.

1929   October: the Wall Street Crash. US loans to Germany are withdrawn.

1930   Nazi vote reaches 18 per cent.

1932   July: Nazi vote over 37 per cent.

1933   30 January: Hitler becomes **chancellor** of Germany.

1934   August: Hindenburg dies and Hitler combines the presidency and chancellor's office. He is now **Führer** of the **Third Reich**.

1936   Hitler sends troops into the Rhineland.

1938   March: Austria becomes part of the Third Reich. September: the Munich Conference. November: Jews and Jewish property are attacked on *Kristallnacht*.

1939   September: World War II breaks out after Germany invades Poland.

1940   Germany conquers Norway, Denmark, the Netherlands, Belgium and France. Germans defeated in the Battle of Britain.

1941   22 June: Germany invades the Soviet Union. December: Hitler assumes direct command of Germany's armed forces. 7 December: Japan attacks the US fleet at Pearl Harbor. 11 December: Hitler declares war on the USA.

1942   The Nazis begin systematic **extermination** of Jews.

1943   January: a German army surrenders at Stalingrad. July: Germans defeated at battle of Kursk.

1944   6 June: the Normandy landings. 20 July: plot to assassinate Hitler fails.

1945   30 April: Hitler and Eva Braun commit suicide as Soviet troops enter Berlin. 7 May: Germany surrenders unconditionally.

Find out more

Books and websites

Hitler and National Socialism, Martyn Whittock, (Heinemann Library, 1995).
The Rise of the Nazis, Charles Freeman, (Hodder, 1997).
The Causes of World War II, Paul Dowsell, (Heinemann Library, 2002).
Witness to History: World War II, Sean Connolly, (Heinemann Library, 2003).
20th-Century Perspectives: Key Battles of World War II, Sean Connolly, (Heinemann Library, 2003).
Witness to History: D-Day Landings, Sean Connolly, (Heinemann Library, 2003).
20th-Century Perspectives: The Holocaust, Susan Willoughby, (Heinemann Library, 2003).

http://db.bbc.co.uk/history/war/wwtwo/
http://www.historylearningsite.co.uk/Adolf_Hitler.htm
http://www.spartacus.schoolnet.co.uk/GERnazigermany.htm

List of primary sources

The author and publisher gratefully acknowledge the following publications from which written sources in the book are drawn. In some cases the wording or sentence structure has been simplified to make the material more appropriate for a school readership.

P9   extract 1 Alan Bullock, *Hitler, a Study in Tyranny*. (Revised edition, Pelican Books, 1962), extract 2 Werner Maser, Hitler. (Allen Lane, 1973)

P11   Adolf Hitler, *Mein Kampf*. (Trans. Ralph Mannheim, Houghton Mifflin, 1943)

P13   Douglas Goldring, *The Nineteen Twenties*. (Nicholson and Watson, 1945)

P15   Ian Kershaw, *Hitler, 1889-1936: Hubris*. (Allen Lane, The Penguin Press, 1998, quoting untranslated book by Hans Frank)

P17   Benito Mussolini, 'La Dottrina del Fascismo', 1932. (Trans. Michael Oakeshott, in *The Social and Political Doctrines of Contemporary Europe*. (Cambridge University Press, 1950)

P19   Stefan Zweig, *The World of Yesterday*. (Cassell and Company Ltd, 1943)

P21   both extracts Charles Bracelen Flood, *Hitler: the Path to Power*. (Hamish Hamilton, 1989)

P23   Adolf Hitler, *Mein Kampf*. (Trans. Ralph Mannheim, Houghton Mifflin, 1943)

P25   William L. Shirer, *The Rise and Fall of the Third Reich*. (Secker and Warburg Ltd, 1960)

P25   Count Harry Kessler, *The Diaries of a Cosmopolitan 1918-1937*. (Weidenfeld and Nicholson, 1971)

P27   Widely quoted; main source Alan Bullock, *Hitler, A Study in Tyranny*. (Revised edition, Pelican Books, 1962)

P29   'I Talked to Hitler', an article by David Lloyd George in the *Daily Express*. (November 1936)

P31   *Adolf Hitler*, compiled by Maurice E. Kelly, no date given

P33   Edmund Blandford, *Under Hitler's Banner*. (Airlife Publishing Ltd, 1996)

P35   Victor Klemperer, *I Shall Bear Witness: the diaries of Victor Klemperer 1933-1941* (Weidenfeld and Nicolson, 1998)

P37   Paul Schmidt, *Hitler's Interpreter*. (Heinemann, 1951); quoted in Niall Rothnie, *National Socialism in Germany*, (Macmillan, 1987)

P39   an affidavit signed by Naujocks at Nuremberg, 20 November, 1945; quoted by William L. Shirer in *The Rise and Fall of the Third Reich*. (Secker and Warburg Ltd, 1960)

P41   Anne-Marie Bauer, interviewed for David Schoenbrunn, *Soldiers of the Night: The Story of the French Resistance*. (Robert Hale, 1981)

P43   Essay 15, 'One Year in the Black Hole of Our Planet Earth: A Personal Narrative' by Rosenfeld; in Dahlia Ofer and Lenore J.Weitzman (eds), *Women in the Holocaust*. (Yale University Press, 1998)

P45   Edmund Blandford, *Under Hitler's Banner*. (Airlife Publishing Ltd, 1996)

P47   Cate Haste, *Nazi Women*. (Channel 4 Books, 2001)

P49   Albert Speer, *Inside the Third Reich*. (Weidenfeld and Nicholson, 1970)

P51   Gitta Sereny, *The German Trauma*. (Allen Lane/ the Penguin Press, 2000)

Glossary

allies countries or groups that fight or work together. The Allies were the countries that fought together against Germany.

annihilation complete destruction

anti-Semitism hostile attitude or behaviour towards Jews

appeasement keeping an enemy at bay by agreeing to some of their demands

armistice agreement to stop fighting, often followed by the end of a war

Bolshevik member of the party, later renamed the Communist Party, that seized power in Russia in 1917

capitalist describes societies in which ownership of industries, etc., is mainly in private hands

casualty injured person

chancellor in Germany, the title of the prime minister; he or she leads the government, while the president is head of state

civil war war fought between people of the same country

collaborators citizens, in countries conquered by Germany, who actively helped the Nazis.

Communism political system where all property is owned by the state and is supposedly used for the common good

concentration camps camps where people victimized by a regime (not criminals) are confined without trial

conservative describes people opposed to, or cautious about, change

corporal army rank between private and sargeant

degenerate not fully human; often just used as a term of abuse

demilitarized an area in which the presence of armed forces is forbidden

democracy government by the people or their elected representatives

denounce accuse

depression long period when trade is very slack because few people can afford to buy things

dictator ruler with unlimited power

disarm reduce the size of the armed forces

dispatch runner messenger

dissident person who disagrees with some government or political party policies

doctrine a belief held by a political or religious group

doss house very cheap place where tramps can stay

economy a country's industry, finances and services

ersatz a substitute or imitation, made and used when the genuine article is not available

exterminate destroy or kill all members of a group

extremist people who favour far-reaching, often violent political or religious action

Fascism describes the political system in Italy, 1920-43. Often used as a general term for all military-style dictatorships with leader cults, etc., including Nazism.

Führer leader, official title of Adolf Hitler

ideologies systems of political or religious thought

inflation rising prices

kindergarten nursery school

left wing describes groups that want a fairer or more equal society

nationalism a strong patriotic outlook, in extreme forms aggressive towards other countries

non-aggression pact treaty in which countries declare they will not attack one another

opulence great wealth or luxury

pacifism the belief that it is always wrong to fight

paramilitaries people who are enrolled in military-style units not attached to the official armed forces

partisans citizens who formed armed groups and fought against the Nazis in countries conquered by Germany

patriotic intensely loyal to one's own country

primary source direct evidence about historical events

propaganda information slanted in order to convince people

putsch sudden attempt to seize power; quickly over, whether it succeeds or fails

radical favouring or intending major, deep-rooted changes

ration a portion or share. In wartime, goods in short supply may be rationed, so that each person can have only a limited amount.

rearmament increasing the size of the armed forces following a period of reduction in armaments

Red used to describe Communists or other left-wing revolutionaries

regime a system of government; generally used of states with dictators or doctrines that limit freedom

reparations payments made to compensate the Allies for damage inflicted by Germany in World War I – Germany was said to be guilty of starting the war

reprisal act of revenge

republic country without a monarch but with an elected head of state (or a dictator)

right wing describes parties and individuals that favour established forms of society, authority and order. Fascism is the most extreme form of right-wing doctrine.

sabotage secret damage done to an enemy's factories, communications, etc.

secondary source type of historical account describing events (for example) not seen by the author

strike refusal to work by a group of employees

Third Reich official name of Nazi Germany; meaning roughly 'Third Empire' it was presented as the successor to the medieval Holy Roman Empire and the German Empire that collapsed in 1918

tyrant someone who rules cruelly and unjustly, with total authority

uprising rebellion or revolt

Index

Titles in the *Witness to History* series include:

Hardback   0 431 17064 9

Hardback   0 431 17065 7

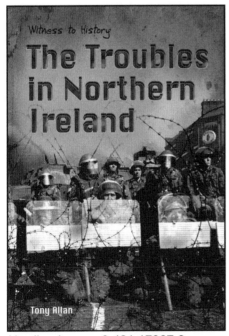

Hardback   0 431 17067 3

Hardback   0 431 17066 5

Find out about the other titles in this series on our website www.heinemann.co.uk/library